Operation New Life

10 Keys to New Life in Jesus Christ

Dominique Danielle Hill

Scripture quotations marked (NIV) are taken from the Holy Bible, New International Version®, NIV®. Copyright © 1973, 1978, 1984, 2011 by Biblica, Inc.® Used by permission of Zondervan. All rights reserved worldwide. www.zondervan.com The "NIV" and "New International Version" are trademarks registered in the United States Patent and Trademark Office by Biblica, Inc.®

Scripture quotations marked (NKJV) are taken from the New King James Version®. Copyright © 1982 by Thomas Nelson. Used by permission. All rights reserved.

Scripture quotations marked (NLT) are taken from the Holy Bible, New Living Translation, copyright ©1996, 2004, 2015 by Tyndale House Foundation. Used by permission of Tyndale House Publishers, Carol Stream, Illinois 60188. All rights reserved.

Scripture quotations marked (NASB) are taken from the (NASB®) New American Standard Bible®, Copyright © 1960, 1971, 1977, 1995, 2020 by The Lockman Foundation. Used by permission. All rights reserved. www.lockman.org

OPERATION NEW LIFE. Copyright © 2021 All rights reserved— Dominique Danielle Hill

No part of this book may be reproduced or transmitted in any form or by any means, graphic, electronic, or mechanical, including photocopying, recording, taping, or by information storage retrieval system without the written permission of the publisher.

Please direct all copyright inquiries to:
B.O.Y. Enterprises, Inc.
c/o Author Copyrights
P.O. Box 1012
Lowell, NC 28098

Paperback ISBN: 978-1-7362921-5-0

Cover and Interior Design: B.O.Y. Enterprises, Inc.
Printed in the United States.

Dedication

This book is dedicated first and foremost to my Lord and Savior Jesus Christ, My Heavenly Father, and the Holy Spirit that is at work within me. I thank you, Father, for your grace that you give so freely, and always providing for me and the boys.

Acknowledgements

I want to thank my boys: D'varian, Dennis, Christian, and Noah. There were times I didn't have gas or food, but you all had provision for the household. I thank God for how generous you all are and ready to give to a need. In the book of Psalms, it says, "Yet have I not seen the righteous forsaken, nor his seed begging bread." We will never be forsaken, God is our healer, our provider, sustainer, and savior. You all have endured my trials and witnessed my growth experience. I am forever grateful and blessed to be your mother. You all have added to my growth in Christ Jesus. I desire to be the best version of a Godly mother for you all.

I also want to dedicate this book to Annee Alexander (Ms. Queen) for allowing me to run alongside you regarding your journey as an author. Seeing you birth, "Prayers and Poetry from the Heart a Spiritual Encounter," and hearing your testimony made it easy for me to put my pen to the pad as a ready writer. I'd like to thank Angel Brown, not only a friend, but a confidant, executive coach, and all the above. You always have a listening ear for me, make time, and always give me inspiring words to bring forth my ideas.

Lastly, but not least, where would I be without my Encounter Church Family? You have built on the foundation within me tremendously. I would like to extend my heart to say thank you Pastors Geoffery & Jasmine Gibbs. Your leadership, wisdom, and love for God's people is indescribable. You both are Great Shepherds from the throne of Heaven put here on the earth to bring forth heavenly encounters to the people of this world. Your hearts are pure and I'm appreciative of every word you both have poured into my family members' lives.

Thank You.

Table of Contents

The Beginning of New Life 9

Operate in Submission 13

Operate in a Renewed Mindset 17

Operate in Your God-Given Identity 22

Operate in the Assurance of God 27

Operate in Mustard Seed Faith 33

Operate in Endurane 39

Operate in Freedom 43

Operate in Obedience 47

Operate in God's Love.. 52

Operate in Victory... 56

A Prayer to Activate New Life.................................... 60

The Beginning of New Life

Operation New Life was born out of frustration in 2016. When you get saved, there are hidden forces that you can't see. Frustration is one of the most prevalent feelings that gives place to negative emotions and behaviors. All of us give place to this emotion at times. If we are not on guard concerning this emotion of frustration, it can produce strife and anger (Rev. Don Loss). I was worn out; do you hear me? My life as I saw it represented burn out, fatigue, aggravation, lack, resentment, and most of all frustration. I felt defeated with no sense of direction, no way of getting off the hamster wheel of my mind. I would wake up in the morning fussing at my boys on the way to school, and still fussing at them while getting out of the car. The same cycles kept following me year after year, until one day I believed it was the road that Jesus used to intersect my life. This is where an encounter with God took place in my life.

One day I had dropped the boys off at school fussing as usual; I didn't even know why to be honest. As I was looking in the rearview mirror, I heard a voice speaking from the inside of me saying, "Dominique, you can't continue like this on this path." I became that woman looking at herself in the mirror and not liking what I saw. God will show you a spiritual mirror of yourself where you will not like what you see. Just like Jesus did to Paul on his way to Damascus, He will do it to you. I knew this wasn't the life my Heavenly Father desired for me or my boys. There was more beyond this life and to this life that I couldn't even see or imagine. No more me being one way at work and drill sergeant mom at home. I began to weep and cried out to the Lord for help, and that is when Operation New Life was conceived in me. I knew I couldn't afford a life coach, so I decided to coach myself to New Life with the word of God. I said, "Father, I need you to operate on every area in me that is not representing you and the life you have called me to."

Like a person who prepares for surgery, new life requires preparation. Jesus spoke this to me in

2016, and I'm now giving birth to what He has put in me. As I am now going through my operation with Jesus Christ, my prayer is that you all will take these 10 Master Keys and allow our Lord and Savior, Jesus Christ, to do an operation on you like never before in your life. Welcome to Operation New Life. It's time you go ahead and pick up these new sets of keys and walk into this New Life in Christ Jesus. I want you to draw a line on a piece of paper and say I'm not going back to this old life. I'm crossing over into the new life that God has called me to. Your operation starts once you realize you no longer want to follow your own way of living. Instead, you decide to follow Jesus Christ with all of your heart, mind, and soul. 2 Corinthians 5:17 (NKJV) states,

"Therefore, if anyone is in Christ, he is a new creation; old things have passed away; behold, all things have become new."

There is no turning back, and there is no getting off the table. You are under a Heavenly Anesthesia. You will have to take your spiritual medication daily, which is the word of God. Will you be ready to be operated on?

My hope for you is that you want to see change in your life, however you will have to do your part. It takes Commitment and Obedience in God's Kingdom. These 10 Master Keys will liberate you from your old life. Do not sit these keys down, carry them with you throughout the days of your life.

Your Kingdom Coach,
Dominique

Chapter 1

Operate in Submission

The first Master Key that will be given to you will be the key of surrendering. In Romans 12:1 (KJV), it says, *"I beseech you therefore, brethren, by the mercies of God, that you present your bodies a living sacrifice, holy and acceptable to God, which is your reasonable act of service."* Operating in the new life that Jesus Christ desires for us, is to recognize that he died for all our sins, so that we can be saved and live our new life in him. Operating the new life in Jesus Christ requires us to surrender the old life that we once knew. Galatians 2:20 (NKJV) says, *"I have been crucified with Christ, it is no longer I live but Christ lives in me."* Our posture of submission should be before the Lord daily. We must tell ourselves we are not going back to the old way of living. We don't want the satisfaction of the world; there must be a desperate cry where we want more of Jesus and less of our earthly selves. We are moving forward in Jesus Christ, surrendering our past over to Him, and allowing God to make all things new in us.

This should be our declaration: Heavenly Father, we give it all to you. We don't want to withhold anything from you. We give you everything that we have identified ourselves with and attached ourselves to. Heavenly Father, we want to be empty before you, we want to be a blank canvas before you, an empty vessel where you can fill us with your desires. This new life is a heart transformation.

> *"Above all else guard your heart for the issues of life flow from it."* -**Proverbs 4:23 NIV**

Transparent Moment

I have struggled with frustration for several years of my life. Frustration comes at times when the outcome of our desires is not in alignment with what we hope to come forth. I was trying to diagnose myself spiritually. Am I cursed? Who sinned between my mother and father? I was like the children of Israel just wandering through life and leaning on my own understanding. The whole time, I wasn't fully committed to God. I allowed my own way to take precedence over what the Spirit of God was calling me to do.

We literally must die to ourselves daily. We need to wake up every morning and say to ourselves; Heavenly Father, have your way in my life today. This life you have given me isn't my own and my desire is for you to order my steps in your word. We need to be broken before the Lord so that He can reconstruct us into His image and likeness, so that His ways and desires will become ours. We need to take a God approach on how to handle the new life, and that approach is in faithful obedience. Our Heavenly Father says we have everything that we need for life and godliness. We will daily lay everything that concerns our life at the feet of Jesus, because his burden is light, and his yoke is easy.

We will surrender the hurts of the old life, so that we can embrace the pain of recovery for the new life that God has for us. Our surrender is nothing compared to what our Lord and Savior Jesus Christ did on the cross 2000 years ago. It's your choice. God will not force himself on you, however He will always be waiting for you. I will leave you with this exhortation: Let God do a mighty work through you and in you. Allow Him to wash you, refine you, and rebuild you in areas where you will be used for good and purposeful work for Him.

Now let us submit and surrender our lives to a good, good Father. His way is better for us. We say, Heavenly Father, not my will, but your will Father. Remember you are not alone in this new life. God is with you always. Embrace His love for you, trust your life with His life that He has prepared for you, and cultivate an everlasting relationship with our Heavenly Father.

Kingdom Coaching Moment

What are you holding on to, that you haven't fully submitted and surrendered over to Jesus Christ?

Chapter 2

Operate in a Renewed Mindset

To operate in a new life in Jesus Christ is to allow your mind to be soaked and saturated in the word of God. We cannot be passive about God's word and use it haphazardly. It is important that we allow our minds to be a Garden of God's Word. Romans 12:2 (NKJV) says, *"Do not conform to the pattern of this world, but be transformed by the renewing of your mind. Then you will be able to test and approve what God's will is-his good, pleasing and perfect will."*

Our minds need to be cemented in heavenly places. Your mind should be like the Garden of Eden where God can walk through it no matter what time of the day it is. Paul's final exhortations to the Philippians in chapter 4:8 (NIV) says, *"Finally, brothers and sisters, whatever is true, whatever is noble, whatever is right, whatever is admirable-if anything is praiseworthy think about such things."*

Take time to center your thoughts on things that fill you with peace and warm your heart. I used to imagine myself in California on the beach of Santa Monica, lying by the window and listening to birds chirping. It brought so much warmth to my soul that I can still feel the joy behind it.

We must take control of what comes in our minds and measure it with the mind of Jesus Christ. Remember we do not wage war like the world does. 2 Corinthians 10:5 (KJV) says, *"Casting down imaginations, and every high thing that exalteth itself against the knowledge of God, and bringing into captivity every thought to the obedience of Christ Jesus."*

To have an operation in the mind that is successful, it will require you meditating in the word of God and have a willing mind to serve the Lord. In the book of Joshua, God told him to *"keep this book of the law always on your lips; meditate on it day and night, so that you may be careful to do everything written in it, then you will be prosperous and successful."* (Joshua 1:8 NIV) It is vital that scriptures become our daily bread.

In the book of Ezekiel, God told him to eat this scroll and to fill your stomach. Ezekiel said, as he ate it, *"Tasted as sweet as honey in my mouth."* (Ezekiel 3:3 NIV) When you eat God's word and let it digest, it is so good. When people talk about the word of God, there is an excitement that comes from His word. I urge you to taste and see that the Lord is good. (Psalm 34:8 NIV)

When operating a new life in Jesus Christ, we need to regulate our thoughts and not allow them to regulate us. The battle is within our minds, that is why we need to fight from a place of victory that has already been won by Jesus Christ. The battleground is not of this earth. We are fighting against forces and authorities, rulers of darkness and spiritual powers in the heavens above.

The enemy desires to take our mind, and if he can take our mind, he can take everything that is attached to us. We fight the battle of suggestions in our minds with prayer and the word of God. Our mouth is our weapon, and we use the word of God as our swords. Speak the word of God in your life and over your family to bring down the suggestions and lies of the enemy. The enemy's goal is to separate us from our identity; therefore, it is vital that our minds be fixated on the Word of God.

Transparent Moment

I had moments where the spirit of heaviness would come over me. I call it the enemy's depression dust. Basically, it is a feeling where you can feel yourself becoming down. The key to combat this is self-awareness of our emotions. That is when I submit and surrender to God in prayer. I put on the garment of praise, and that is when an exchange happens from God. (Isaiah 61:3 KJV)

Your emotions can affect your thought pattern. Do not follow the street called Emotional Lane, because it will lead you nowhere. We can feel our emotions, but do not follow them. I repeat, do not follow, because they will lead you into a ditch. I have said some hurtful things that I can't take back, all because I allowed my emotions to control my thoughts, and my thoughts controlled my response. Remember you have complete control over your mind shifting off Jesus Christ.

Allow the word of God to permeate in you, so that you will be able to fight off the suggestions of the enemy in this new life.

In the book of Matthews, Jesus answered Satan by saying, *"It is written man shall not live on bread alone, but on every word that comes from the mouth of God."* (Matthew 4:4 KJV) When the enemy comes with thoughts that are not in direct alignment with what our Heavenly Father says, you say, "For it is written, get behind me Satan," and use your mouth to declare the word of God. We don't have to let thoughts torment us. The weapons we fight with are not of the world. On the contrary, they have divine power to demolish strongholds. We will commit ourselves to thinking thoughts that are Heaven focused, and not earthly focused. This is where you shift your thinking into Kingdom Thinking, covering your head with the Helmet of Salvation.

Kingdom Coaching Moment

Recognize the thoughts that are not aligned with the word of God. How can you cultivate your mind into a Garden of God's Word?

Chapter 3

Operate in Your God-Given Identity

The new life requires you to operate in your God-given identity. Who do you say you are? Are you aware of your spiritual lineage? Your DNA is not even of this earthly realm. Knowing who you are and whose you are is an area that God will reveal to you in this operation. He will examine you to see what areas are not in alignment with what He created.

Genesis 1:27 (NJKV) says, *"So God created man in His own image; in the image of God He created him; male and female He created them."* You are made in the image of the Almighty God. You come from a culture that is not of this earth. Come in agreement with God through the power of Jesus Christ that you are attaching everything that God says you are in Him.

Identity is equivalent to purpose. We all have purpose here on this earth. We don't recognize that until we submit and surrender our full selves to our Heavenly Father. We live in a world where we measure ourselves against other people, and we covet the things and the appearances of others. It's like we have put ourselves in competition with others. God is not calling us to compete with one another, but to love and serve one another.

In the old life there were pieces of your identity taken from you, which left you walking around broken and confused. You no longer have to wander, being lost and confused. Allow God to shape you in the way that is best to Him. Jeremiah 18:6 (NJKV) says, *"(Insert your name), can I not do with you as this potter does?" Declares the Lord. "Like clay in the hands of the potter, so are you in my hand, (insert your name)!"*

Transparent Moment

When I was younger, an adult called me and my siblings ugly. I remember going home and praying to God to make me look like Janet Jackson. From that moment I knew I was ugly. Even though I didn't actually know what ugly was, I fit the description. In middle school, I couldn't hang around a certain group of girls because I was flat chested, and I was still wearing braids with beads, so I began taking my beads out of my head in gym class. In my teenage years, when a guy would break up with me, I automatically assumed it was because someone else was prettier than me or I was skinny. Missing pieces were taken from me as a child that led to my insecurities as a woman.

In my twenties, I'm battling with insecurities within myself. I began looking to everyone else to point out the qualities in me and the direction for my life. I would associate my identity with my career. I remember I was going to become a dental hygienist because someone said I looked like I should be a dentist. I was basing my identity on people's perception of me. I was looking for my identity in work, not in the one who created me. My Pastor would say, "When we forget who we are in Jesus Christ, we quit pursuing what belongs to us in Jesus Christ. We seek meaning and purpose in horizontal things because our identity isn't vertical" - Pastor Geoffery Gibbs Jr. of Encounter Church Charlotte.

One afternoon, I was listening to the Yolanda Adams show on the radio, and she said, "Don't ask people, but ask God what your purpose is." When I heard that, it was like God was speaking to me, because He saw my frustration with life and me asking everybody except Him.

What I know for sure is we don't need to look to others for validation, but to our Heavenly Father who knows us even to the very little hairs upon our head. Our Father is our creator, and you need to know that you are creative, full of power, and full of love. When God made you, He said this is very good. (Genesis 1: 31 NKJV) The makings of you are beautiful, everything about you is wonderful, you are fearfully and wonderfully made. (Psalm 139:14 NKJV)

Acts 17:28 (NKJV) says, *"For in Him we live and move and have our being."* You are distinctive, intricate, unique, and creative. You are powerful beyond measure, you are fearless, courageous, and called to do great things. You have spiritual birth rights in the Kingdom of God, so rise up in your rightful identity.

God is the creator of all things. He makes all things out of love, and that is beautiful. Allow God to remove the false labels that you and society have placed on your identity. Take those generic labels off now and understand that you are a beloved child of God. Let God's word be a reflection of who you are in Him.

Kingdom Coaching Moment

Are you walking in a form of mistaken identity that is not mirrored in the image of God?

Chapter 4

Operate in the Assurance of God

Do you trust the Heavenly Father to give you a new life? There are times we allow our earthly experiences with trust to affect how we place our trust in our Heavenly Father, and we doubt God when it comes to our entire well-being. Let's be honest, we know what the word of God says, but do we really believe that He will meet all of our needs in that moment?

Trusting in God is knowing that His outcome is best, even when our desired answer isn't given. Jeremiah 17:7-8 (NIV) says, *"Blessed is the one who trusts in the Lord whose confidence is in him. They will be like a tree planted by the water that sends out its roots by the stream. It does not fear when heat comes; its leaves are always green. It has no worries in a year of drought and never fails to bear fruit."*

Operation New Life requires you to put your life in Him and leave it there. I need you to catch the visual. Pick yourself up and everything that you are carrying and leave it with Him. Trusting God requires you to start building a relationship with Jesus Christ.

> *"For I know the plans I have for you, declares the Lord, plans to prosper you and not to harm you, plans to give you hope and a future."* **-Jeremiah 29:11 (NIV)**

We can't just read the Word of God and not make it applicable to our livelihood. The cares of this world will have us hyperventilating and falling prey to doubt and fear. We have to understand that our Heavenly Father desires to give us His best.

The Holy Spirit dwells inside of you. He will be your tour guide here on this earth. It's vital that you yield to Him so that He can lead you into all truth. Allow your spiritual roots to grow deep within Him, so that you can be firm and immovable in Him. Jeremiah 1:5 (KJV) says, *"Before I formed thee in the belly I knew thee; and before thou camest forth out of the womb I sanctified thee, and I ordained thee a prophet unto the nations."*

Wow, our Heavenly Father already appointed our purpose. We don't have to look for it, He has already established it. He is our promise keeper, He will never fail us, and His word is true. Our Heavenly Father never sleeps nor slumbers. His eyes are always upon us. Numbers 23:19 (NIV) says, *"God is not human that he should lie, not a human being, that he should change his mind. Does he speak and then not act? Does he promise and not fulfill?"* Trust God to operate on and in every area of your life. In God you will never be impoverished. He is the source for all things that we need for life and godliness. (2 Peter 1:3 KJV)

Transparent Moment

I fell ill on September 28th, 2019, and the night before, God gave me a vision of me walking through my hallway, and there was so much resistance trying to keep me from moving forward. I kept speaking the word of God, no matter how strong the force was coming at me. I just kept speaking God's word out of my mouth.

The word was I woke up that morning, still perplexed about the vision, but didn't know that the vision would serve as a warning for what was about to happen.

About 8:30 a.m., I began to lose feeling in my legs and arms and immediately called 911, however, I didn't panic. I was calm and assured that God was with me. I kept speaking God's words. I kept saying under my breath, "I have no reason to fear the Lord is my Light."

They rushed me to the hospital and hooked me up to the monitors. My mother in-law and my son were with me. I felt something in my lower ribcage begin to shift, like something was locked in a chamber. At that very moment, I ushered my son and my mother in-law over, because my life started to dissipate out of me.

In that moment, I knew I was leaving this earth and I wasn't afraid. I trusted that my Father would be with me even unto death. God allowed me to see in two seconds what my life here on this earth would have looked like. All the things that I thought were important during the course of my life, none of it surfaced. The only thing that flashed before me in that moment was my children and brother, who would've been getting out of prison and waking up to the fact that I'm not here on this earth. God stopped death and time.

The beauty in all this was that the monitor wasn't even picking up what was happening in the spiritual realm. The Breath of Life was leaving me, and it was so pure, and the length of it was as long as my index finger. When you speak the Word of God, it's the breath of our Heavenly Father that moves you here on this earth.

This is a reminder that this life isn't our own. We live out of the breath of God, and as my dear friend Angel says, "It's borrowed breath." Just like Shadrach, Meshach, and Abednego, they trusted God would save them from the blazing furnace. Jeremiah 17:7 (NIV) says, *"Blessed is the one who trusts in the Lord, whose confidence is in him."* Once you understand what is in you, you will learn to operate differently in the New Life that is given to you by our Lord and Savior Jesus Christ. Trust in His unfailing love for you, and that He will never fail. There will be no need for you to add worry to your life. Your soul is anchored in Him and you surely will not drift away.

Kingdom Coaching Moment

What situations in your life have made it hard for you to trust in the Heavenly Father?

Bring those situations to the surface, and trust God with the outcome.

Chapter 5

Operate in Mustard Seed Faith

Operating in the New Life that God requires of you is going to take mustard seed faith. It's vital that you exercise your faith muscle. We live by faith 365 days a year, 7 days a week, and 24 hours a day. Hebrews 11:1 (NKJV) says, *"Now faith is the substance of things hoped for, the evidence of things not seen."* This life we live will require us to walk by faith and not by sight. Hebrews 11:6 (NKJV) says, *"But without faith it is impossible to please him, for he who comes to God must believe that he is, and that he is a rewarder of those who diligently seek him."*

You have to believe and trust that God's word is true and it's settled in you. Faith comes by hearing, and hearing by the word of God. (Romans 10:17 NKJV) Faith isn't a carnal way of thinking, where you just go jump and believe that all will be well with you. Faith is believing in the word of God alone. You have to hold on to the confessions of what you believe, and not waver.

We must understand our timing isn't God's timing and He doesn't move on our frequency. We go wrong when we question the hand of God, when understanding the presence of God is connected to the hand of God. God is always with us, although the solution may be delayed in our view. Our Heavenly Father is always on time. God said to Paul, *"My Grace is sufficient for thee."* (2 Corinthians 12:9 KJV) You are well equipped and able to hold on to the promises of God.

Transparent Moment

I used my faith to have a supernatural childbirth. In my first three childbirths, I used an epidural to help me with labor pains. The side effects led to me having back problems, and I knew I didn't want to go through it again. Having an anesthesiologist sticking a needle in my spine was a dreadful image in my mind. I knew I wanted to have my son naturally, and I believed that I could do it.

I was given a book by a dear friend called *Prayers and Promises for Supernatural Childbirth*. I began to condition myself with the word of God regarding pain over the course of 6 months. I looked at the cross and saw the pain Jesus Christ bore for me on the cross. I began to align my prayers and the prayers in the book to build my faith and trust in Jesus Christ to be with me. Every day I would thank Jesus Christ for the pain that He bore for me on the cross and believe that I could bear the pain to bring my unborn child into this world naturally.

On October 23, 2012, it was time to give birth and my doctor kept asking me, "Are you sure you want to do this?" I was completely sure. As my labor pains intensified, I kept thanking Jesus for dying on the cross for this pain. I remember feeling like I was about to pass out as I laid down on the table. The next thing you know, my water broke, and I pushed out a 7lb 2oz beautiful baby boy.

The experience serves as a memorial stone in my life to represent how Jesus Christ helped me to endure the pain of childbirth. We must believe that everything is possible for one who believes (Mark 9:23 NKJV). Believe the supernatural for your life and that God will use unprecedented experiences to bring about His purpose. You can do whatever you put your mind to; there is nothing too hard for our Heavenly Father. All you need is mustard seed faith to move any mountain in your life. We can do all things through Jesus Christ who gives us the strength to do so. (Philippians 4:13 NKJV)

Faith is knowing that God will provide for you no matter what the natural circumstances are screaming at you. Faith is believing that your needs are already met before you can even see it. Faith is believing that you are already healed before you have seen your healing. Faith is believing that we have been redeemed and bought with price. Faith is believing that God will never leave you nor forsake you. Faith is believing that God will forgive you of your sins. Faith is knowing that you are loved with an everlasting love. Faith is knowing that you can't do anything without Him. Faith is believing and understanding that you are not of this world. Faith is knowing that nothing can separate you from the love of Jesus Christ. Faith is knowing surely, He will rescue you and protect you. Faith is believing what God has for you; it is for you. Faith is believing that this too shall pass, (whatever your *this* is).

Faith is moving beyond the natural state of being. For example, food is scarce, and we have just a little bit of money on hand. Our minds are consumed with the coming days and weeks ahead, and we are worrying about our tomorrows instead of living in our today. The Bible says,

> *"Therefore I tell you, do not worry about your life, what you will eat or drink; or about your body, what you will wear. Is not life more than food, and the body more than clothes? Look at the birds of the air; they do not sow or reap or store away in barns, and yet your Heavenly Father feeds them. Are you not much more valuable than they? Can any one of you by worrying add a single hour to your life?"* **-Matthew 6:25-27 NIV**

God gives us enough for our today; My dear friend Ilycia would always tell me, "there is purpose in your today." The word of God is like hidden treasures within our souls. Know that Jehovah- Jireh will provide for you.

Kingdom Coaching Moment

Take a moment to examine this season of your life and the things God has called you to do. Have you allowed fear to fog your vision of the supernatural being possible in any area?

Chapter 6

Operate in Endurance

Operating in this new life that Jesus Christ called you to will call for endurance. Endurance means the ability to withstand hardship. *"Consider it pure joy, my brothers and sisters, whenever you face trials of many kinds, because you know that the testing of your faith produces perseverance."* (James 1:2 NIV)

It is imperative that we finish our race strong, remember there were giants of the faith in the Bible that ran their race without giving up. *'Therefore, do not cast away your confidence, which has great reward. For you have a need of endurance, so that after you have done the will of God, you may receive the promise."* (Hebrews 10:35-36 NKJV) In this life, you have been given a race only you can run; our race is how we live our life in Jesus Christ. We all will have different life paths; however, we all are pressing toward the common goal, which is to live in eternity with our Heavenly Father. *"Therefore, since we are surrounded by such a great cloud of witnesses, let us throw off everything that hinders and the sin that so easily entangles. And let us run with perseverance the race marked out for us, fixing our eyes on Jesus, the pioneer and perfecter of faith."* (Hebrews 12:1-2a NIV)

Your audience is in Heaven, not on this earth, so allow your training to come from the throne of Heaven. We need God's spiritual food that will provide us the substances we need to continue in this marathon. The race will come with distractions and hurdles, and you must be very careful that you are operating in the spirit of discernment. There are people who are sent to push you off course and cause you to be concerned with things that don't serve your purpose.

> *"Trust in the Lord with all your heart and lean not on your own understanding; in all your ways submit to him, and he will make your paths straight."*
> **-Proverbs 3:5-6 NIV**

Even in the hard times of despair, God will make your paths straight. The Bible says, *"There is a way that appears to be right, but in the end it leads to death."* (Proverbs 14:12 NIV) You must continue the way God leads you along the journey. You have to make sure you resist, withstand, and recover from any setbacks. You are Heaven bound which is your high calling, so set your mind on things above as you run your life's race with all strength and power from our Heavenly Father.

Don't give up! You have been empowered by the Holy Spirit. Push through the trials of life with the word of God. Philippians 3:14 NIV says, *"I press on toward the goal to win the prize for which God has called me heavenward in Christ Jesus."*

"Running with the Giants" by John C Maxwell, talks about the Old Testament heroes and what they would have wanted us to learn from them. One of the heroes is Esther. In her section, she talks about how God has a place for us, and that no place is out of place when you're in God's place.

No matter where you find yourself in any season of life, just know you are in your starting position to go forward in Him. He gives us new mercies every day. (Lamentations 3:22-23 NKJV) Now I'm passing the baton to you. Go run your race!

Kingdom Coaching Moment

What challenges are you facing in this life's race? What are you willing to leave behind to press toward the high mark in Christ Jesus?

Chapter 7

Operate in Freedom

Operating in freedom starts with Jesus Christ and ends in Him. God is our Alpha and Omega and everything in between. Freedom is being free to live the life that God has called you to live here on this earth. You are free from the works of sin when you accept Jesus Christ as your Lord and Savior. John 8:36 NIV says, *"So, if the son sets you free, you will be free indeed."*

Break free from the shackles of this world.
Break free from self- sabotage.
Break free from other people's opinions of you.
Break free from the demonic strongholds.

We are free to walk worthy of the calling God has placed in us. Our Heavenly Father has given us authority and dominion over the earth. You have the resurrection power on the inside of you to loose the chains off your life and your children's lives. Take advantage of that power!

Come out of hiding and step into the river of the living water that freely flows with no end. There is a part of yourself that is deeper than anything this temporal world can provide. Where the Spirit of the Lord is there is liberty. (2 Corinthians 3:17 NKJV) Step into God's reality of liberty for your life. In the presence of God there is fullness of joy. (Psalm 16:11 NKJV)

Transparent Moment

I was liberated by the Holy Spirit on April 4th, 2020. God had shown me I could create the life he desired for me. I was liberated by someone else's testimonies. He literally removed the scales of self-sabotage from my eyes. It was like a voice asking me…

> "Who told you, you have to live a conventional life that you succumb to? You don't have to force yourself to be at a workplace that doesn't fit who I created you to be."

Just like God asked Adam and Eve, "Who told you, you were naked?" when they hid in the Garden of Eden. (Genesis 3:11 NIV)

For the last seven years of my life, I have been going from job to job trying to find my fit in the workplace. The truth is, I don't fit. I felt like God gave me the clearance to move forward in the direction of where I knew He was calling me.

God didn't create us to be ordinary, but to be and live extraordinarily lives here on the earth. Just like Moses when he was born, the Bible said he wasn't an ordinary child. I'm here to let you know that you are not ordinary. You are filled with God's treasures on the inside of you and He is waiting for you to discover them.

Do you remember the Sesame Street song? "I got a new way to walk, (walk walk), I got a new way to walk (walk, walk) and my walk suits me fine." That is what I am experiencing in this season of my life, a new way to walk. I'm walking this earth in FREEDOM that my Heavenly Father has given me. Where the Spirit of the Lord is, there is liberty, and since the Spirit of the Living God lives in us, we walk in freedom, in step with the Holy Spirit.

Kingdom Coach Moment:

In what areas of your life do you need God to liberate you? My prayer is that the Holy Spirit will reveal the area or areas to you and give you a new vision to clearly see the freedom that He has for you in this life.

Chapter 8

Operate in Obedience

Use your ears to be obedient to God's word. *"Be quick to listen, slow to speak, and slow to become angry."* (James 1:19 NIV) Faith comes by hearing and hearing the word of God. (Romans 10:17 NKJV) For God to change us from the inside, we must believe in His word along with applying it to our lives.

Jeremiah was appointed as a prophet to the nation of Judah. He was sent by God to bring a word to the people; however, they didn't listen, and they rebelled against the word of God. This is another great example in the Bible given to us By God to learn from.

Looking back in my old life, I shut my ears off to people who had my best interest at heart. This is an area that I can say I have full experience with. I will admit, I'm not a good listener at all, and my boys tell me, "Mom you are not listening." I never had a mirror to see what proper communication looks like. I believe it led me to be a poor listener in the natural realm and spiritual realm. It led me to make poor decisions, which was a result of not being able to provide for my family and acting out of disobedience. Further complicating things, I got married based on my emotions rather than getting the clearance from God. God sent people to give me wise counsel, however, I had already made up my mind that this was what I was going to do.

> *"Where there is no counsel, the people fall; but in the multitude of counselors there is safety."* **-Proverbs 11:14 NKJV**

There is a kingdom within us that needs to be overthrown with the Word of God. God sent Jeremiah to go to the nations and kingdoms to uproot and tear down, to destroy and overthrow, to build and plant. (Jeremiah 1:10 NIV) In the same manner, God is calling me to bring a word to His people. He has called me to tell them there is a new life that requires faithful obedience in Jesus Christ, and there are invisible kingdoms within us that need to come down in the mighty name of Jesus!

In this season, let's choose to let go of what we want to hear and allow the Holy Spirit to guide us into all truth. We are going to take desperate precautions in this area when we feel the gate of defensiveness come out, or when our spiritual antennas are not catching the signals of Heaven because we want to lean on our own understanding. We must also watch out when our will becomes objective to God's will, and we need to look back at the cross. Jesus Christ's obedience to our Heavenly Father's will is the perfect model for us to follow.

We have to do things differently in this new life; change begins within us. This new life will require your obedience and faithfulness to God. God may use someone else to deliver His word to you. Don't ignore that person like the nation of Judah ignored Jeremiah or like I ignored those sent to me. Instead, make sure that your heart is operating in purity, so that you will be ready and able to receive. Psalm 51:10 NIV says, *"Create in me a pure heart, O God, and renew a steadfast spirit within me."*

Listening helps us hear and understand the will of God. You may be asking yourself, "How do I hear God?" You find Him in His word. Hebrews 4:12 NIV says, *"For the word of God is living and active sharper than any double-edged sword, it penetrates even to dividing soul and spirit, joints and marrow. It judges the thoughts and attitudes of the heart."* We have to walk in the spirit and allow our souls to be chained to the word of God. Pause for a second and visualize your soul being chained to the word of God. See your soul being eternally bound to His word. That is the safest place our souls will EVER be!

Whatever it takes to obey the word of God, we want to obey out of our love for Him. Think about how Jesus Christ went to Calvary for each one of us. I like to make it personal, so I say to Him, "I owe you my obedience Jesus. Thank you for doing something I know I couldn't have done."

It's time for us to mature in the word of God. We are no longer babies, and we need the meat and potatoes of the Word to grow. Growing leads to us becoming doers of His word. James 1:22 KJV says, *"But be ye doers of the word, and not hearers only, deceiving your own selves."*

Kingdom Coach Moment:

In what areas of your life do you struggle most regarding obedience? How could your relationship with God help you win the struggle over this issue?

Chapter 9

Operate in God's Love

Operating in new life requires us to operate in God's love. It's a love that symbolizes sacrifice, forgiveness, and mercy. *"For God so loved the world, that he gave his only begotten Son, that whosoever believeth in him should not perish, but have everlasting life."* (John 3:16 KJV) Our Heavenly Father shows us His love every time we wake to a new day. God's forgiveness is His love to us, and God holds no record of wrongs. *"Love is patient and kind. Love is not jealous, or boastful, or proud."* (1 Corinthians 13:4 NLT)

Our life is a representation of God's love for us. God created the heavens, the earth, and mankind out of love. The Bible says that God is love, and if we are imitators of Jesus Christ, then we must love like Him and not like the world. Our love can't be self-centered or based on conditions that we are accustomed to. The same unconditional love that He shows us, we must show to others.

> *"You have heard that it was said, 'Love your neighbor and hate your enemy.' But I tell you, love your enemies and pray for those who persecute you, that you may be children of your Father in heaven."* -**Matthew 5:43-45a NIV)**

This love isn't feeling based, where you pick and choose who and what you want to place your love in. This love is powerful, and full of mercy and grace. I love how the story in the book of Genesis illustrates how Adam and Eve represent God's love for them. Even in their disobedience He still loved them. He gave them fig leaves to cover themselves; they felt shameful. Despite their disobedience, God was still concerned about their feelings towards their nakedness. Even in all of our mess and filthiness, our Heavenly Father accepts us just as we are.

Transparent Moment

I have personally mishandled the word love in my own life. While growing up, I thought love was a feeling-based emotion. In my childhood, I was never told I love you by my parents unless I said it first. To be honest, I said the L word to everyone I dated (not proud of that). Do you see how emotions like to disguise themselves as love?

Love is an action word and God has demonstrated His love for us. It's a love that is known and that we can read about. God loves us with an everlasting love, a love that is incomparable to what this world can bring. When we come to God and ask for forgiveness, He celebrates us and makes us new in Him. Just like the prodigal son in the book of Luke who sinned against Heaven and his father, yet his father accepted him and had compassion on him.

Earthly relationships will have us feeling like all love is lost and that there is no coming back from a heartache. I'm here to tell you God's love never fails us. God's love will not break our hearts. He will not let us down, and He will not let our foot slip. Place your heart on God's heart and allow it to get lost in Him. Can you imagine and visualize that picture of an indescribable love that has no boundaries?

"I pray that out of His glorious riches He may strengthen you with power through His Spirit in your inner being, so that Christ may dwell in your hearts through faith. And I pray that you, being rooted and established in love, may have power, together with all the Lord's holy people, to grasp how wide and long and high and deep is the love of Christ, and to know this love that surpasses knowledge—that you may be filled to the measure of all the fullness of God." (Ephesians 3:16-19 NIV)

Pursue your King Jesus with all of your heart, mind, and soul, and you will experience His unfailing love, where in turn, the fruits of the Spirit will come forth in your life.

Kingdom Coach Moment

Do you need to check your love engine? Is your engine operating in God's love or the world's love?

Chapter 10

Operate in Victory

Operation New Life is a life of victory, not defeat. As a matter of fact, let's go ahead and change your name to Victory. You will wear the name Victory. It is stamped and sealed in you. John 16:33 NKJV says, *"These things I have spoken to you, that in Me you may have peace. In the world you will have tribulation; but be of good cheer, I have overcome the world."*

We can rejoice in knowing that we are already triumphant over the cares of this world because of our Lord and Savior. *"And the Lord is the one who is going ahead of you; He will be with you. He will not desert you or abandon you. Do not fear and do not be dismayed."* (Deuteronomy 31:8 NASB).

Victory means: the overcoming of an enemy or antagonist, according to the Merriam-Webster Dictionary.

The enemy is already under your feet, a defeated foe. The Bible says in Luke 10:19 KJV, *"Behold, I give unto you power to tread on serpents and scorpions, and over all the power of the enemy: and nothing shall by any means hurt you."* That is something to rejoice about! We have victory because of Jesus Christ. Understand what is in you, the power of the living God. No giant, no devil in hell, no sickness, no disease, nothing shall overtake you. Understand that the Lord Jesus Christ is our shepherd, and He guides us into all truth.

In the story of Jehoshaphat, several camps came to declare war upon him. Jehoshaphat knew that the army was too strong for them, so he called upon the Lord and they declared a fast amongst the people of Judah. This is what the word of the Lord said, *"Do not be afraid or discouraged because of this vast army. For the battle is not yours, but God's."* (2 Chronicles 20:15b NIV) Our God is our defender, our strong tower, our shield, our buckler, and He encamps all around us.

Transparent Moment

I began experiencing some rebellious behaviors from my son out of nowhere. This behavior went on for 8 months. My son was headed for destruction to the point of death. I knew as a mother I had to continue praying for my son. I had to keep loving him, even in the pain that he was causing. I began to change my attitude about my son coming in at five o'clock in the morning. Every time I heard a knock, I thanked God for bringing my son home.

When you are a mother, no matter what your child may do, your heart is extended with love because our Father shows us the same unfailing love, grace, and forgivingness. At that moment, I knew I couldn't fight that battle. I had exhausted all of my know-how. I began to battle with anxiety. I couldn't sleep. My nights and early mornings were spent praying for my son's safe return. A wise mother told me to give him back to the Lord and trust God will intervene. I did just that, and on March 25th, God stepped in. Yes, it was unbeknownst to me. No parent likes to see their child taken away. I was faced with what I wrote about: Do you trust God even when the outcome doesn't meet your expectations?

Every day I trusted God with my son and for his release. I had an army of prayer warriors praying and standing with me. The Bible says, *"Rejoice always, pray without ceasing, in everything give thanks; for this is the will of God in Christ Jesus for you."* (1 Thessalonians 5:16-18 NKJV) Trust in the Lord and His unchanging hand, He is always for you.

There will be opposition that will come against you. Just remember to preserve in prayer and keep moving. *"If God be for us, who can be against us?"* (Romans 8:31 KJV). Continue to walk in victory, and remember you wear the name victory. DON'T take it off. Remember there is a place beyond victory called Triumph.

Kingdom Coaching Moment

In what areas of your life are you not claiming VICTORY in Jesus Christ?

A Prayer to Activate New Life

Thank you, Jesus, we come to you with our hearts wide open. We call on the name of Jesus Christ our Lord and Savior at this moment now. Heavenly Father, we thank you that your ears are attentive to your servant. Forgive us for our sins we have caused known and unknown. I lift up my brother and sister to you. We desire to operate in a new life in you. We are calling on your name now and I ask that you come and do a mighty work in the lives of your people. We are desperate for change that only you can do. We are a blank canvas before you; color our life how you desire Jehovah God. You are the great I AM, the King of Kings and the Lord of Lords. You are sovereign, you are merciful, and you are an amazing God.

Heavenly Father, we thank you for who you are, we thank you that you are God alone and there is none like you. We make you bigger in our life, we make room for you to come and make your home in our hearts. Heavenly Father, it's your desire that no one shall perish, but to be saved by your son Jesus Christ. Heavenly Father, we are withholding nothing from you, we are exchanging our lives for the life you have for us. Change us; make us more like you. We know that all things are possible in you.

Heavenly Father, we thank you for your word that you send out, and knowing that it doesn't return back void, it accomplishes what it was sent to do. God, I ask that you do a transformation in the life of the person that is reading this book.

Heavenly Father, I ask that you heal your sons and daughters from all brokenness, all pain, all addictions, all malice, all oppression, all depression, all sickness, all diseases, and all relationships that don't glorify you. Heavenly Father, we surrender it all unto you now. Heavenly Father, you said that your burden is light, and your yoke is easy. Jesus, we know that you are with us, you walk with us in every storm and situation. Even now you are moving on their behalf; even now you are bringing them into new life. Heavenly Father, we thank you for the living water that you are. I pray Father that whoever is reading this now will come to you for nourishment. I pray that an increase in thirst and hunger for righteousness will spring up in them. May the God of hope fill you with all joy and peace as you trust in Him, so that you may overflow with hope by the power of the Holy Spirit. May you continue to carry your keys into the new life that Jesus Christ is calling you to.

In Jesus Name.

Amen.

CPSIA information can be obtained
at www.ICGtesting.com
Printed in the USA
BVHW060408040521
606341BV00002B/702